Gandhi the Messiah

A book of poetry by

Rajeshwar Prasad

TSL Publications

First published in Great Britain in 2023
By TSL Publications, Rickmansworth

Copyright © 2023, 2025 Rajeshwar Prasad

ISBN: 978-1-912416-70-7

CONTENTS

5

The Birth of Gandhi

God surely incarnates for liberation
In this wide world – the earth of only mirth
To abolish evils after vacation,
That is a rotation to clean the earth.

Gandhi takes birth, and the aim was divine –
To end evils overloaded by the people –
To make the entire world a pure shrine –
To abolish violence was nev'r here simple.

He's for love, peace, ahimsa, tolerance, and truth;
For breaking up the chains of slavery in India –
For removing the sufferers from the dearth –
For the sake of humanity with His blissful idea.

Satyagraha was only one weapon in His life,
And the rulers faced freedom strife.

Porbandar in Bliss

With Gandhi's arrival on Earth, came bliss
To Porbandar, was fully revealed –
No people in the condition to miss –
All woes and sorrows were veiled.

People assembled there to see His look
And sang and danced in His house happily;
Noted it in their heart and mind's book,
That was felt by others completely.

"He has come to our land to send away –
To abolish the evils of the world –
To restore peace, love, and justice in any way –
By the right means of truth and ahimsa fold."

They enjoyed His incarnation
As they witnessed after duration.

The Divine Light

Gandhi's birth brought the divine light to Earth
Which spread in South Africa and India.
In the course of time, He turned the mirth
Into bliss, expecting also in Asia.

His arrival as a full tide of the sea
To clean all the past dirt from the world's face.
He well began the humanity plea
To restore love, ahimsa, justice, and peace.

His sincere love for all animals and birds
Like all human beings as they are weaker –
Indeed they are Nature's true friends –
And are better than man, and meeker.

Now men act only for gain in their prime;
And virtuous work has become a crime.

The Madeira War

Gandhi met Gokhale in England, so far
On debate and called Him to discuss;
Reaching He knew about the Madeira War –
So, he thought to work in the then fuss.

He got the training and passed the test;
He was in the post of Sergeant
All the team were with Him with chaste;
He with all others did for achievement.

But after some time He knew about it;
The role of the trainers was prejudiced;
Colour was then the main thing to cheat
So it was disliked by them to be tied.

He decided to depart from the war
Because of the racialism to bother.

Always Human Practice

Being a barrister, He did human law
Found on the pages of Nature to Deliver –
To go forward for it on the Truth vow;
Not to practise the art of a cleaver.

He read human nature to handle;
The black deeds of human beings to control –
The courtyard of law to make a model,
While all others were there for the money roll.

He took the minimum fee for His advice
And all others took it as a surprise.
But He never thought of such a good price.
However, they, then, felt they were too wise.

Activities must end with virtuous gain,
Otherwise, all practices are in vain.

Gifts That Gandhi Gets

The gifts Gandhi got were a matter of debate –
Either to keep or to give – right or wrong,
Gifts of thousands but a burden, no rebate –
So, none should blame Him without knowing.

All praised His true service to all humankind –
From terrace to floor, moved the whole night
Because all His ideas were too kind,
But as dawn approached it got the light.

His children told Him to forget all this
And Kasturba was totally against this will.
The impression was, He was not ready to miss;
He against Kasturba attempted to drill.

They agreed to leave all presents;
He decorated His soul and all its sets.

When He Escapes

Gandhi reach'd South Africa for a bar practice
To work in favour of humanity
While all others began to criticise
He tried His best for divinity.

The Whites attacked and beat Him also.
So He took His shelter in a friend's home
Where the police said to escape to grow –
To avoid violent attacks in the room.

He chang'd His clothes, a scarf on his head
And guided by them he escaped from there.
Whatever was then for Him in His need
To protect Him from cruel deeds to dare.

He reached the police station to set
Where no one, then, could detect.

For Plague Victims

Madanjit said to Gandhi about the outbreak
Of plague in an indentured colony;
Writing to Him in a pencil note, for the sake,
And He soon went to serve them, not for money.

He, Godfrey, and Madanjit began to work
To save their lives as the Whites were away
The plague had made their future dark,
But they chang'd from deep dark into bright day.

They held them in a go-down as a hospital,
And they served them as their kith and kin.
Hydropathy saved only some mortal
Out of twenty-six, in the plague to win.

The human services in His every pulse,
While some people felt all this was a curse.

The Zulu Rebellion

The Zulu rebellion against the then-rule –
They boycotted the newly imposed law.
The police beat and killed them as a mole
There was none to take them out of the flaw.

No one to serve them or put balm on wounds
While they were gentle, ignorant, and calm.
The reign suppressed them as if they were hounds;
Police dealt with them as angry beasts and warm.

Only the union of Gandhi served them;
All Whites were there only to see
From the black grill and then went to claim
That they were masters – in the fates of thee.

The team came as a heavenly relief;
The Whites behaved with them, with complete belief.

The Boer War

Gandhi formed a great union of comrades
And got its services accepted as a corps.
The British completely threw away His plans,
But Booth supported it for its regards.

They secured certificates of fitness.
Escombe and Laughton supported the plan;
Outside the firing line with kind-heartedness
But at a critical moment within the line.

They moved nearly twenty-five miles a day
Bearing the wounded men on stretchers' racks.
They carried Woodgate on the way –
The corps was disband'd after six weeks.

Their work at the time was much applauded
And the Indians' prestige was much aided.

Balasundram's Case

Balasundram was victimized by one,
Who was white in colour, and great of honour.
There was the chance to be helped by none
As he belonged to a man of black colour.

His master beat him – broke his teeth enough
As he was an indentured labour
And for Indians there, everything was tough;
No one was for him in his neighbour.

He came to Gandhi, and was taken to hospital;
A case was lodged against his master
And the judge found him guilty to settle
But Gandhi said only to escape from there.

Thus, He became the sufferers' hero
While the Whites' motive became fully zero.

The First Night in Phoenix

He read "Unto This Last" on the journey
And decided to practise in His life.
He established it, which was so thorny;
Whatever was possible in strife.

The ideals of the book were followed;
The first night very much tiresome for Him;
The engine to print the paper failed;
He at that time worked the whole night with them.

The Phoenix Farm supplied the paper
At the right time because of their night labour
That left its mark in His heart deeper –
He did in His whole life as its keeper.

They settled on the way to Sarvodaya
That was like changing night into day.

We Will Not Submit

September of nineteen hundred and six –
The Jewish-owned Empire Theatre was full
From floor to ceiling with Indians to fix –
To decide, the Asiatic Law was a lull.

In every face full expectation
To be new, to be done, to happen,
Which is considered a resolution
Expressing solemn determination.

The determination was not to pay;
The resolution had been passed
They decided to delay it anyway
To boycott the law as it was housed.

Gandhi attempted enough to abolish it
And so taken aback by the government.

West and Polak

Two white men from Gandhi's family lived –
West, pure, sober, God-fearing and humane,
A dinner companion of Gandhi was mixed
In a vegetarian restaurant which was run.

West offered his service to plague victims,
But Gandhi said, "You are not needed here."
Polak, a young man, was impressed by deeds
Who saw Him off at Johannesburg to fare?

Polak gave "Unto This Last" to Gandhi to read
During His train tour to catch as the crane.
He did so and felt its complete need
And stored it in His deep brain.

Soon He made it true at Phoenix Farm
Where everyone could flourish without harm.

Gandhi Comes as a Tide

With Gandhi, the tide came to Indian politics;
Others went aside, to work as His aides –
They all worked hard on the ahimsa tracks
And Gandhi was their leader with ample sides.

Gandhi had His own new way of going ahead,
Where no one had taken a dip to debate.
But He moved forward and got a stead
To deal with the foreigners for rebate.

He broke all the past records of solution
And through the ahimsa arm He got freedom –
Proving the value of the Satyagraha motion –
Possible only because of His wisdom.

Only one who did so for the country
And who award'd solution as a sentry.

Indigo Stains

In Champaran, an old system of indigo –
Run for centuries by the masters
Of the planters, necessary to grow –
In three kathas out of twenty by planters.

No solution was seen by them, no idea
But Gandhi rescu'd them by visiting their doors.
Abolished the evil of tinkathia;
He washed the indigo blot of the farmers.

The reign and masters attempted their best
To obstruct His movement for a solution –
To misguide from the evils was the rest,
But He worked with them till their abolition.

He washed away fully the indigo stain;
And He left Champaran showing His brain.

The Gandhi-Irwin Pact

Gandhi began talks with the Raj to settle;
Spanned a sixteen-day time to face;
Lived in a Muslim's home to battle
That was five miles from the table place.

From there Gandhi went to the Viceroy's palace
To talk with Irwin about India's rebate.
Some days performed the routine twice
And walked back to report the fate.

"Indeed a seditious Middle Temple,
Now posing as a fakir in His garments
Was striding half-naked up the steps
In the Palace to parley on equal terms."

The Gandhi-Irwin pact was signed;
The Raj agreed to release all imprisoned.

Gandhi Visits Haridwar

Gandhi visited Haridwar during the holy Kumbh fair
The Shantiniketan team was present too.
The Phoenix team was also there
To serve the visitors, not to boo.

Gandhi arrived and lived with others –
Many people visited Him for His look
On the ghats, as the *Father*, and none bothers.
With no time to eat, He only shook.

On His long journey, all around Him pain;
In the scorching, sun, He tour'd for there.
This was the real way of devotion
Everything was too bare at the fair.

People had only to fulfil formality.
Indeed, they had no faith in divinity.

Savarkar Refuses

Savarkar came from jail after clemency;
Then Gandhi called him and said to condemn
But he refused and moved his fancy
Not ready to pay for the nation's main.

After this, he didn't look at Him
For his whole life, and began a mission.
Did he want to reduce the *Fame* to dim? –
To move against the outcastes' vision?

Savarkar made a group to go against Him
So that he and others would repeat the past –
The red past of a thousand years of their cream,
Which they never wished in any way to last.

He took rest only when he finished the deed
After twenty-six years of his plot fuelled.

Gandhi Himself Slaps

Gandhi was on a freedom journey for Gorakhpur
With Kasturba and Mahadev on a night train.
His tour was as a third-class passenger
And many ideas were flooding His brain.

At night He wanted to sleep for sometime
Because of His drowsi- and weariness;
The heavy crowd saw Him as their prime,
He could not sleep and felt then restless.

He could not tolerate such a disturbance;
Became angry with Himself for His deed;
To control anger He slapp'd to face;
Three times heavily as an urgent need.

Other passengers witnessed and said,
"O Bapu, what are You doing? You're our Dad!"

The Dandi March

After midnight in a marching camp chest,
Where Bapu with all others was taking rest –
The police team came to Him to arrest
As the time after midnight was the best.

The police flashed their full light in His eyes
To get Him risen, while He was sleeping.
"Do you want Me?" "Yes, under the clause."
"Get up soon, be ready to go with a gang."

"But can you Let Me brush My teeth?"
"Yes, You can brush, but as soon as to go."
He did, kept His bedding in a breath.
Before it, He bent and sang "Vaishnav Jana Ko".

With the police he departed for jail;
But Ambedkar was in a move to derail.

Bhagat Singh's Fate

Thousands were unhappy with the amnesty
As it didn't apply to all prisoners;
While Gandhi bargained, with honesty
For their release – for Bengali jail goers.

Bitterness because of Bhagat's death sentence
Along with Sukhdeo and Rajguru for relief,
Who were the accused in Saunders' killing case –
With the loss of three, India has lost its belief.

While every point, Gandhi bargained hard;
Irwin was adamant and rejected
The clemency of Bhagat and his own ward,
But to gain mercy for three, Gandhi failed.

Neither Bapu nor the Working Committee
Had made it a breaking point for thee.

Ambedkar in the Conference

Gandhi said, "I desire to turn Delhi's truce
Into a final settlement for freedom;
But for heaven's sake, give a frail man's grace,
Sixty-two years have gone, a little chance."

The master refused to spell out a time
For freedom or awarding grace;
Gandhi insisted He leads the state in His prime
While Ambedkar said that he came to face.

Ambedkar criticized Gandhi enough
For not frontally attacking casteism
Without feeling the task was very tough
And wished a solution to anger reform.

Ambedkar advocated only rights.
He had held how many independence fight?

Gandhi in England

In England for independence to gain –
With a team to take part in the debate.
But all His attempts to gain went in vain
As Ambedkar there made a loose rate.

There he said Gandhi does not represent;
Others were there to show the diversity
And all homely ideas to stop a rebate,
So failed to keep the vow of unity.

He wished Ambedkar to be silent –
To discuss the internal point at home
After returning and gaining the best;
But his ideology was tame.

So He arrived without home rule;
Others only blamed and hunted mole.

Gandhi and Ambedkar

Coming from England, "a show" in Bombay –
Between "he" and "He" – too-bitter a clash –
A result of his apathy and no ray
Of solution for the blot of the top class.

Ambedkar wanted the solution
Of the untouchability stigma
In one moment race as a magician
But that seem'd an unpractical dogma.

Became angry and decid'd to convert
From Hinduism to Buddhism to be free;
With many untouchables to end the blot;
From a thousand years' blot as a referee.

Forgetting his Hindu-fold made proud too cold;
Without thinking and unpractical hold.

Gandhi and Bose

Gandhi involved Himself in the Congress;
The choice for Nehru's successor was Subhas Bose
Who was the hero of the young minds –
Who wished Hindu–Muslim unity in gross.

Bose presided at the Haripura Congress;
Was also the chairman of the party,
But held sympathy for the Nazis' race
That was against the Indian polity.

"A known enemy is better than an unknown one."
Bose had his own path to secure freedom
That Gandhi ignored saying "pre-war-done" –
A rehearsal for the civil war custom.

He escaped from his home for a rebate;
Unknown what happened to his fate.

Muslim Patriots

Azad, a Muslim and true nationalist;
Sikkandar followed his ideology
Marooned Ansari, was not the nastiest –
Tried to save it from Jinnah's divide-o-logy.

Ghaffar and his brother from the Frontier State
Better than any other of India's fate –
And attempted hard for India's rebate,
But her division on the divine date.

Many Muslims played their role for freedom;
Completely against India's division.
Some wished her partition using wisdom,
While some attempt'd for the same union.

Alas! Jinnah was not a man to listen
And the partition came as his passion.

Harilal to Hiralal

"It has become hard for Me even to live.
How much pain you are inflicting on us
In the last phase of our life? At last save;
Your present deeds break My heart in pieces."

"The powerless voice like wounded mothers
Will surely stir someone's heart to deliver."
"God can work wonders – sinners into saints;
Nothing will please Me better than to bear."

At last, he reconverted to Hinduism.
"Ba, I've brought this orange only for You."
"And anything for Me?" Bapu asked him.
"No, nothing for You as you have by Her."

"Oh, there's no doubt of it of your view. Know!
But now, do you want to come with us?" "No."

Yervada Again

On the fourth of January, the police for arrest;
Devadas roused Gandhi at the Mani Bhawan.
"Please pardon Me if I offended you in the past."
As She thought they might never meet again.

"Thousands of rupees for one race meeting!"
The award was announced for the clash.
So Gandhi decided for resisting
As the separate electorate to harass.

Soon, for curse to boon, Gandhi held a fast;
The leaders of the untouchables gathered
Round the mango tree, and signed the pact –
Separate seats within the bound as cluster'd.

The agreement was cabled to London;
For MacDonald and his ministers to sign.

Calling Harijans

From September nineteen thirty-two,
Began the call "Harijan" for "untouchable"–
Proposed by a reader of Navajivan, too –
He was also untouchable.

Reminding caste Hindus of their black deeds –
They heavily heaved on the Harijan's head.
He blessed in the assembly two bills
In favour of them, who're treated like dead.

"Socially lepers – economically slaves –
Religiously denied – they'd spirit like God.
A Hindu lawyer says – doctors serve to save;
But Brahmins didn't officiate acts; so sad."

While they were quite able to hold all,
Their blott'd deeds had made them fall.

The Quit India Movement

Cripps' fiasco inspir'd the idea to go.
The Committee declared "Quit India".
It's eighth of August nineteen forty-two
At Gowlia Tank in Bombay for the idea.

The Muslim League did not join the movement.
On the ninth of the month, many were arrested;
The Congress was bann'd from the settlement.
Though a number of meetings were held.

The movement jerk'd the root of the empire.
There was bloodshed and violence everywhere.
In four days, six hundred men were to the pyre.
Gandhi was leading from the jail to pair.

It was quite clear that they had to quit
Yet only for some time, Indians had to wait.

Kasturba Tells Sushila

Arresting Kasturba and Sushila to detain;
When they were brought to the railway station –
They were detained there for the next train
But others seem'd in a different condition.

She looked at the people passing there –
Hither and thither and for their own work
The situation was entirely bare –
And many other leaders were in the dark.

"Sushila, do you see all this here and there?
We're under arrest, people are busy on their own.
Bapu's in jail, while others are free
And the time for the nation is none."

Bapu was in jail with others to gain
While others didn't think for the nation.

Kasturba Dies

It was Shivaratri – the nineteenth of February.
She began to cough enough in the jail –
She died on the freedom journey
And got from the black hall jail, only wail.

On the lap of Gandhi, She took Her last breath –
Red and dark tears from Gandhi's eyes for Her death.
No remedy was given to save Her breath,
While Gandhi wrote many letters in His full faith.

The prisoners got Her bathed with Him –
Her elements were covered with the shroud
Made of yarn spun by Bapu as Her dream
The funeral march was conducted by the crowd.

Prisoners cremated Her in jail
Who sacrificed life for slavery to derail.

Gandhi Behind Bars

Two months' imprisonment in the Transvaal
For not show'ng His registrat'on in Natal;
Again three months' imprisonment in the Transvaal;
Arrested at Palm Ford, and then on bail.

Again arrest'd and released on bail;
At Volkhurst arrested and sentenced.
In Champaran served with a notice, but not jail.
Once at Palwal, and in Bombay released.

Arrest'd near Sabarmati for writing articles;
Arrested at Karadi and was sent to harass.
Again in Bombay and sent to Yeravda cells;
Once again for His march towards Ras.

At last, imprisoned for "Quit India" –
All''s well – thirteen times for His Truth idea.

Arrest with Mahadev

On the ninth of August nineteen forty-two;
He along with Mahadev was arrested.
On the way to the car, Narayan came too,
Who kiss'd him, and asked which he acted?

"Yes, we will meet again in free India."
Narayan said to meet him in the free state.
But he pass'd away leaving this idea
In the Aga Khan Palace without any rebate.

His dead body was also cremated there
Where no kith and kin could participate.
The prisoners took part in his rite with a dare –
Of the funeral march to go ahead to date.

With Mahadev's death, Gandhi fully lost his right hand
And since then He was fully in another's band.

Godse with Thatte

On the tenth of July nineteen forty-four –
Godse with Thatte went to Him with a dagger –
The police noticed and moved to batter
And arrested them to ensure the place fair.

The police asked about the cause of it.
"Yes, once Gandhi will be shot down by the man."
The police re-asked the main cause to meet.
He replied shamelessly without wan.

They wanted to obstruct the meeting
Of the viceroy regarding the matter.
But He was to go ahead for getting,
Which was disliked by them, but better.

Their mission was to continue their race fair,
Conducted by them, guided by the top chair.

Savarkar's Group Disagrees

The group of Savarkar disagrees more
Than any other group of his set against Him.
When Gandhi announced to talk at Jinnah's door,
Godse and Thatte tried to end Gandhi's dream.

In Sevagram, they too wanted Him to end
From leaving for Bombay to go for talks.
They arrived at the entrance to send.
The police arrived, but they said for their ends.

On their refusal to leave the centre,
Godse and Thatte were then arrested.
A dagger was found on Thatte to share.
They said that a martyr would find Gandhi dead.

"That will be too great an honour for Him
And Godse will stop Gandhi's movement to freedom."

Nehru as Successor

Gandhi declared Nehru His successor
On the fifteenth of January, forty-two –
"Neither Patel nor Rajagopalachar" –
And Nehru will wonderfully lead, too.

"India'll defend herself through the ahimsa arm.
Thus, a messenger of peace to the world;
Nehru will do quite well for the peace charm,
Who will always work against the war fold."

Nehru was an Oxford student and young too.
While Patel was old, ill but nationalist;
Nehru was socialist and young to do;
Patel also felt Nehru was best.

The new engine was fitted to further
And Nehru accepted it as a debtor.

A Letter to Hitler

"Dear friend, many have been urging Me to write
To you only for the sake of humanity.
I resisted because of feeling right
That, and from Me, an impertinent duty."

"Something tells Me, I must not calculate
And must make appearance for the worth.
You, the only one in the world for debate
To push all mankind to savage for mirth."

"Now, must you pay the price for an object;
However worthy, it may appear to be?
Will you hear the appeal of one to date? –
Who has deliberately shunned? Thee!"

Gandhi wrote it in the name of Hitler;
As he's a danger to the earth's matter.

Do or Die

The arrest of Gandhi, nationwide wave of fury;
Village after village – town after town –
Found heroes willing to defy, disrupt, and be fiery.
The government killed six hundred men.

Several pockets declared themselves free.
The doors of the factories were locked.
Indians streamed, shouting "Do or Die!"
Arrests, beating, and bullets countered.

Some rebels were machine-gunn'd from the air.
Lacs were jailed for indefinite terms;
The eruption was crushed then and there.
The Raj's property was damaged by worms.

It was the most serious rebellion;
Some were non-violent for the union.

Britain Will Quit

On the twenty-fourth of January nineteen forty-six;
Only a month before the mutiny;
A private telegram from London to fix;
Sent three ministers to leave their colony.

To negotiate a settlement of the point
On the nineteenth of February announced
By Attlee, "Britain has decid'd to quit"
In the House of Commons, so some fancied.

"If India elects for independence,
She has a right to do so for her sake.
So the mission came to India thence
To transfer power for India's make."

Many talks later, they quit India,
Which was the Empire Foe's longstanding idea.

Attempts on Gandhi's Life

Gandhi toured Panchgani in the summer
In Sahyadri hills for His recovering –
For a complete three weeks, He stayed there;
Attempted in the train in which He was touring.

Bumped against the boulders, kept on the rails,
Between Neral and Karjat railway stations.
He slept right through the bump and repairs,
Learnt only the next morning in durations.

Alas! Know! What a black attempt on His life
Had been plotted by the darkest devils
With the dark old ideas with a violent knife
Only to enhance the paternal evils!

"Man ever lives in the jaws of Death.
Dead when Death closes its jaws. Is it no Faith?"

In Sweepers' Colony

Gandhi stayed for talks, not in a palace,
But in a shed of a sweepers' colony
In Delhi with His team for independence
There's no point in conversion as Yeoli's funny.

Tried hard to save from partition,
Some others attempted hard to gain.
As a result, Congress accept'd division –
In this mission, Jinnah was to bargain.

The interim government was to announce;
The leaders came to gain His blessings there;
Cripps and Lawrence went after the truce
And He said to them to work for the poor.

Such a great Man who lived in such fame
Only to encourage them to end the shame.

Gandhi in Bannu

Ghaffars were no less than other patriots
Than those of Hindu nationalists of India –
Who had an approach with its own merits –
Thought for United India, a great big area.

It was, really, Ghaffars' concurrence –
Who regard'd Gandhi with every breath of life;
Who invited Gandhi to visit their province;
Gandhi went to end the partition strife.

On the way of His tour, Khudai Khidmatgars
Were present to welcome Him heartily
With their bows and arrows, not as wonders;
Others in the community behaved dirtily.

Ghaffars were in favour of United India,
All patriots supported their idea.

The Partition of India

Partition came from the womb of freedom
On the eve, when people were to enjoy.
All tried to save it using their wisdom –
But because of a few, they all lost their joy.

Freedom came on with both joy and sorrow
And filled up tears in the leaders' eyes.
The principal cause of their own woe –
Which was long since past in mind diaries.

Some leaders willed to fulfil their will –
To divide the motherland in pieces.
Gandhi tried to save it from the division reel.
But others did not let Him continue.

In the holy brow of India, the black blot
Which could not be ignored, was lost.

Others' Role in Partition

He focussed His attention to stop –
To restrict the partition as was dosed
There was a full chance for it to drop.
Some others didn't help, so He was bother'd.

"First to cut out Me, then divide India."
Firmly, attempted hard to convince, then.
Others didn't listen to Him for such India
While others continued to work with such men.

Someone for Bengal – Ambedkar for Mahad –
Jinnah for Pakistan and Savarkar was a seed
To try to show that Gandhi represented
Not all of India but a small part, indeed.

Thus, the purity of India was robbed
By many, and so she at last too sobbed.

The Last Fight against Partition

"Indeed I am after all a gambler."
He said after the "Three June Partition Plan".
But no promising signs were seen by her.
He hunt'd for likely allies for the plan.

Some socialists were still willing to stand up
As were Hindu nationalists like Tandon.
Some Hindu politicians in Sindh set up;
Muslim leaders in north, He, not alone.

Suhrawardy and Sarat Bose sought a free Bengal.
But Nehru, Patel, and the Committee reject
As many leaders of the Congress drill,
But Gandhi wanted to recognize the state.

Not united independent Bengal,
But the partition made India mortal.

Riots in Delhi

The winter approached and advanced –
Of uprooted and unprotected ones –
Hindus, Sikhs, and Muslims in camps shivered –
People killed them in their hospital rooms.

Passengers were stabb'd, thrown into a river;
A man was kill'd while opening their little shop
Where he repaired spectacles ever.
Refugees were butchered and had no hope.

All happened because of different faiths,
And none because of any wrong committed;
Allowing or silent onlookers for deaths.
Such was the condition of the time shed.

Leading the world to non-violence,
Then blood and knife were like a concurrence.

Gandhi Puts out the Fire

He put out the fire of riots in full flame;
Whenever He went, people were quite silent
They followed Him, and they didn't blame
As it seemed, everyone was His client.

The riots in the Noakhali area of Calcutta
Where thousands came to the hot soil easily;
Began to shiver the brow of Bharatmata
And the earth bed looked entirely bloody.

He moved among them without any fear
To pacify them to change their angry heart –
To restore peace in the heart-broken tear,
So everyone could clean minds and body dirt.

Both communities were pacified;
All easily felt but, before it, many died.

Only Three Alive

In Srirampur, only three were alive
After the riots held by the Muslims there;
All others were killed in a violent drive –
Hindus' houses seemed a dreadful fair.

Gandhi made a cottage in Srirampur to live
Near the trees of palms; lived ninety days;
He put out the fire of flame on the sleeve;
Not very easy for others in such ways.

Muslims came and repented their deeds,
They said not to repeat it in future.
Some women were restored to their faith,
Many lived with Him as He was their dear.

Such was He who restored peace and rest
In the lap of thunder where none was chaste.

Move Alone

"Move alone" was announced at Kazirkhil
For helping the local Hindus after the riots.
Each party to a different village to drill –
To give challenge through ahimsa for fights.

Pyarelal took on Bhatialpur as was windy;
Sushila set up a clinic in Changigaon;
Amtus Salaam based herself in Sirandi;
Sushila Pai in Karpara for peace going on.

Kanu went to Ramdevpur to hold a programme –
His Bengali wife Abha went to Haimachar;
Prabhudas accompanied by Sarat and Parshuram;
And Gandhi Himself would go to Srirampur.

Thakkar Bapa also did the same work for fame,
Which was necessary for the area of shame.

Hemant's Donation

Hemant, a feudal lord donat'd his lands
To Gandhi for setting up a charitable trust;
Who gave attorney power to Charu's hands,
Who made a centre to meet the harmony thirst.

Many women from Calcutta's elite families
Had based themselves in Noakhali villages.
Ashoka Gupta camped in Tumchar for changes;
Hundreds had gather'd momentum to wash rages.

Followed the advice of Gandhi to work
Which was then not possible by other
As the situation was too tense and dark
And the distinction was much too bitter.

Thus, Gandhi put out the violent fire of riots
Through non-violence to end the then fights.

Adopted Villages

In Bhatialpur, all the Muslims pledged
That they would risk their lives to protect
And do their utmost to get the wealth robbed –
And abducted women restoring to date.

An idol was restor'd in a temple;
Sushila's work was well seen in Changirgaon;
Looted goods were return'd to Hindus, well;
The weekly market was reopened then.

Kanu Gandhi organised group activities
To lower the bar between Muslims and Hindus;
Amtus and Bapa also did several works;
Even Sirandi's Muslims took the pledges.

They said to defend the right of Hindus
To practise their faith in quite fearless ways.

Evils or Devils

Godse went to Sevagram for the motive,
Who was a member at different times,
Of two large Hindu groups to conceive
An idea of violence like the communal wines.

Godse, Apte, Bagde, Kistayya, Karkare and Pahwa,
Who processed guncotton slabs for the deed –
Who wished to wash away Truth and Ahimsa –
Who desired to remove Truth or Lord?

Behind them a big team and ideology,
Who had practised only to blame, then –
Who fulfilled only their mythology –
And the honour of India to blacken.

They fully killed Truth and nonviolence
By using their weapon of ignorance.

Freedom Arrives Well

Fifteenth of August nineteen forty-seven –
A day for India of joy and sorrows,
Which arrived after years from heaven;
And from its womb also permanent woes.

Freedom came, but lost some parts of the past –
India and Pakistan – two separate states –
After the long disturbances came at last –
Leaving no chance for several debates.

Gandhi tried His best to maintain unity,
But failed as none were ready to forge ahead –
Others served their interest in beauty
To maintain their old monopoly with heed.

Jinnah for Pakistan – Ambedkar for Mahad –
Some for small Bengal – some for Hyderabad.

The Interim Government

Twenty-four of August, the government was made,
Then the most difficult task of the day.
Otherwise, freedom was to be delayed,
If differences continued in the way.

Nehru, Patel, Prasad, Das, and Sarat of the Congress
And the Dalit leader Jagjivan also held;
Asaf Ali for the Muslims in the race;
Ali Zaheer and Shafat Ahmed Khan to shed.

Sikh leader Baldeo, Matthai, a Christian
And a Parsi Bhabha was on the council.
Azad was President of Congress then,
So said to accept a Congress list – Hindu all.

Gandhi was noticed, but sought no advice;
Nehru and Patel did, which led Wavell ready to face.

Jinnah and Pakistan

Jinnah us'd to attract hundreds of men,
But later changed his fold to Pakistan
As several said for a separate nation
Which Jinnah sounded those to embrace in.

"Must think, why is India, not nation one?
Was it not one during the Mughal period?
Is India two or only one nation?
If yes, why not many more too, or the third?"

Jinnah continued to bargain for it
And declared a "Direct Action Day".
Many Indians participated in to fit,
But none could find a solution in any way.

Fazlul Haq moved a resolution
And the honour of our India was torn.

India of Gandhi's Will

Gandhi wanted to make India of His will –
India as the alone world and to see,
Where Sarvodaya was possible and evil nil
To set the way for equality to be.

His experience in Phoenix flashed Him,
Where none tried to further the mission,
While the knowledge of others was too dim,
And no will to maintain His revision.

India secured its freedom through Him.
His only mission was to further it
For peace, truth, love, ahimsa, and justice to
mean.
But all the evil-doers did not set.

His mission and vision were darkened then
Without shame by the black will of men.

Lok Sevak Sangh

At one time, Congress was irrelevant
And Gandhi wanted its abolition soon
So that none could defame its vent and art;
And so He felt Lok Sevak Sangh was a boon.

He advocated its establishment
On the national level – its units everywhere –
In each and every village for nourishment
As no one was then to do this with a dare.

For its members, coarse clothes are necessary
To wear, its wings would be at a level;
Duty to develop within its boundary.
This would be a well-ideal world sample.

Its constitution was made by Him,
But assassins caused His plan to dim.

The Village Reign

For the development of India well,
The rule of the village was quite necessary
As without it none was able to dwell
A good chance for the welfare of the country.

If each and every hand gets to work for him
There would be widespread progress;
Then the regular progress of handloom
Would soon award employment as the grace.

He advocated the village reign for good
Of the country where everyone would think
For himself far better to go ahead
So the progress of His light would not sink.

Without it, everything was treachery;
Annihilation was compulsory.

God's Reign

Gandhi always proceeded for God's reign –
The rule that would be commanded godly –
There would be love, peace, and rest – no woe sign –
Where all mankind would live humanely.

There would be chastity, joy, and regain;
They would be ruled by ahimsa, love, and peace,
Where there would be no difference to gain –
Between weaker and stronger in any source.

There would be affinity to every one;
Divine bliss would be showered by God;
Hate, envy, and lust in the heart of none,
With no ray of sorrow on the ground.

The same reign as is in God's kingdom,
And possible only thorugh Gandhi's wisdom.

Nazism and Fascism

Returning from England, Gandhi reached France;
He wanted to meet Mussolini to know
How his cruel mind was born in the Fascist face –
And about Germany's Nazi show.

He met Romain Rolland in this regard,
Who said to stay away from Mussolini
And his "ism" – for His country award.
Otherwise, he would be like an enemy.

He said it was the worst in the country;
Nothing was in the name of humanity;
Jews were victimized by the sentry;
And ism's full force against divinity.

Fascism and Nazism thrilled the soul
Of humanity to make the world foul.

Faith in Indian Civilization

The changes in Europe that had taken place
Was also possible in India it was said
And when big change would take its clean face,
India would be destroyed beforehand.

"In Europe for progress is an illusion –
Our social setting is thousands of years old.
We survived in our civilization;
Our faith is turning in another fold."

"The war between God and Satan forever;
Either, we fight with the Westerners
Or adopt them heartily and to cheer.
We must not copy the Western in the open."

"European civilization is a Satanic charm;
We should be godly and rooted in calm."

Satyagraha

For world peace, Satyagraha is the best weapon;
Gandhi had full faith in it, He nurtured
It was an absolutely innocuous way as seen;
He was aware of it, and it fostered.

"Man can only make an honest attempt
God is the awarder of the result;
On the clean way of God, nothing can tempt;
And no one pays for this consult."

"Faith overtakes everything in the way
To gain each thing for our earthly pleasure
For all the works, be crystal clear like day;
Pleasure providing us without measure."

"Satyagraha gives us a full crystal clear light
Which one can use in a spiritual fight."

Love to the Motherland

His love for India was utmost and got it free –
There was no more than Him, who had loved her.
He stood as an overgrown banyan tree,
He had, in any way, no sign of bar.

Sacrificing his entire life with bravery
To the service of the loving motherland –
For liberation from the chains of slavery;
Tackling the British with His ahimsa hand.

He went ahead to clutch the foreigners –
To get them out of the field of India;
Written on pages in golden letters;
Not by arms or swords, but by an idea.

Ideas liberated His motherland,
Impossible by any other hand.

Truth

Gandhi views that "Truth is God and God is Truth";
Sure! Truth never dies, as God is not to die.
Truth is divine light, it is not dearth,
As universal beauty is never to lie.

Truth's a Tree with the fruits of God;
The finest engine to pull mankind well;
Taking man out from evils for brotherhood;
A place where one can take an interest to dwell.

Aha! Truth is followed through love divine;
Truth is fully identical to God;
The path of Truth is for the brave alone,
Never for a coward in anyone's mood.

Truth gives us everything that is not won
And all the hidden facts that were unknown.

Ahimsa

The man who doesn't follow the religion
Of ahimsa, in his life, was always simple
Has no right to show himself as a man
Or any of a religious disciple.

Truth lives in protecting as visions;
The stronger should protect the weaker ones
As ahimsa is the root of all religions
And should be followed in all conditions.

Ahimsa gives birth to love, peace, and full bliss –
Ahimsa creates the ground of fraternity –
Ahimsa gives a broad way never to miss
That is the main thing about divinity.

Ahimsa is the virtue of all religions,
Propagandized by all the missions.

Service

Service, His religion in commission;
Also in omission and in His pulse –
In His bidding speed as His vision;
Failure to His service was a curse.

Whenever a chance to be a self-server;
He did not miss such a golden chance
And served a sufferer or a leper
Or any in bad condition to glance.

A man without true service is a machine –
A man without love is an inanimate thing –
A man with this passion is like a shrine –
A man without ahimsa is a pathless being.

Man is recognized for his duty,
And duty increases his beauty.

Swadeshi

Gandhi was always against foreign-built things;
But against the wild works of a machine
Making all humans dependent beings,
All technical products were to shine.

Beginning the swadeshi movement widely;
Focusing His long sight on employment
Of a maximum of men to spin broadly,
To give work to the hands for settlement.

Swadeshi was like Nature – self-acting
In the basic nature of all mankind –
And encouraging hand spinning
For saving man from such an evil mind.

Swadeshi stood for the final emancipation
Of the human soul from its earthly mission.

Sarvodaya

Sarvodaya, a linked part of Satyagraha;
Satyagraha is only possible when peace is in the nation;
Sarvodaya, one of the fruits of the messiah;
Ahimsa is a fruit of meditation.

India's a poor country – a well-known fact;
None tried to know the curse of poverty –
The fine way of its removal was tact –
A few moved to abolish this dirty.

Without the Sarvodaya plan, no chance of joy
In India in any condition, in any way;
Gandhism can only cleanse the dirty ray –
Which can certainly change night into day.

Without Sarvodaya, no welfare of India
And for its welfare was shown this idea.

Home Rule

A wise person doesn't attempt a bigger bite
Than he can digest – well acknowledged.
Full independence, something infinite –
Or superior to home rule, He too said.

"One step is now enough then we'll further;
Do not become the prey of any idea;
And the way of home rule will be better;
So no one will hate and harm our India."

"Gradually, we must further our mission
To gain home rule and to break the main chain,
Otherwise, the chance of major division
And our hands will be void for fun."

"The only way to attain independence,
Which can be well done with our confidence."

Non-cooperation

Gandhi's really loyal to the government;
The events of nineteen hundred nineteen;
That disillusioned Him for a new bet –
To gain justice and pleasure for all men.

He became a full non-cooperator;
The Rowlatt Act, the Jallianwala garden
The Khilafat had taken a long tour –
And He was changed fully as the warden.

Inaugurated on the first of August
Of nineteen hundred and twenty;
With Congress also to approve it
In the Nagpur session for liberty.

The aim of home rule was re-affirmed
And power also confirmed.

Sacrifice

Sacrifice is an active link to the welfare
Of others done without any will of it –
Either temporal or spiritual nature –
But no return for it or dare to fit –

It does have thought and word, as well as deed;
Others embrace not only humanity
But all life – not according to one's need
From the standpoint of non-violent duty.

Not the sacrifice of weaker animals' bare
Even with a view to serving humanity
Must be an act that conduces the welfare
Which engages the will of divinity.

A body is to be cherished, surely;
We realize our right place to God purely.

Eat to Live

Eat to live for the country and humanity;
Do not live to eat to be a burden;
Strengthen already the weak chastity;
And remove the long slavery curtain.

He simplified His food as far as possible;
From kingly food to uncooked fruits;
Which was always easily available;
That could be consumed as edible roots.

Sure! His health was sound, unlike others.
Firstly refused, but later accepted
Said by doctors to take of goat mothers
While other types of milk were rejected.

Wishing to live, not to eat but to serve,
That was then written deeply in His nerve.

Fasting

Fasting was a weapon that He used
For His sake or against the unjust rule
That Indians liked to see refused –
That was against the land and its people.

In His life He practised it many times
And compelled the Raj to go back soon
As the reign of slavery was like their fines.
His fast was for all Indians a boon.

Fasting is not for those who have a wrong desire
Rather for those who have a virtuous will –
For those who have a strong will like Shire –
For those who were helpless and unable.

Fasting enables one to gain that is undone
And its need and strength are felt by one.

A True Vaishnava

A true Vaishnava is mov'd to others' woes –
Helps people in distress – who has no pride;
Respectful to each; ill of none he thinks;
Whose humane-feeling dimension is so wide?

Who self-controls his action, speech, and thought;
Twice bless'd a mother, who bore such a one;
Equal see'ng – another's wife as mother, a sight,
Who utters no untruth or gets a wealth of none?

No impact of attachment is in him;
He himself the centre of pilgrimage;
Who deals with rapture only to God's name;
Without cunning and greed as a sage.

He is purged of anger, desire or none;
Thus, he really is a true Vaishnava man.

Decayism

A number of "isms" in the world we see –
One of the isms was in the Godse's blow,
Only full faith in violence to agree;
Which does not believe in virtue to grow.

This violent "ism" occurred over long days
Until thirtieth of January, forty-eight,
It was flourishing for twenty-six years
Which did not let one see the Truth gate.

Came to light with the assassination
Of Gandhi, the world's greatest (or unlike) man;
Such type of man was not in any nation
His works for humanity were a fan.

This "ism" killed the world's universal Truth;
After Him, nonviolence lost its faith.

Fadeism

This "ism" came into light after the release
From jail of Andaman after clemency;
He had in his heart one thing not to miss;
That was running in his mind as fancy.

He formed a group, a community,
He formed a big organization;
That had nothing to the divinity;
That had only one idea, to miss the Man.

Begged for his clemency, and releas'd from jail;
The Raj admitted his plea for release;
Came out and began to derail;
Tried hard to get success in his pledge.

Only one motive to stop the mission
By Him, which was His welfare commission.

Know Savarkar!

Know Savarkar! Who issued "Abhinav Bharat"
In London with fine writings and speeches.
Some youths were attracted to it;
And joined in anti-British activities.

Did he participate in the deeds done?
Were all satisfied with him then?
He decid'd to do something as an Indian.
Escaped from hands, but was arrested soon.

He begged for clemency when in Andaman
With a term not to go out of Ratnagiri range.
Later, never did nor joined any Indian
In any works for freedom. Had he rage?

Know, jumping was a revolution by him?
Begging made him gallant (or a maxim).

Godse's Attempt in Panchgani

Gandhi went to Panchgani to recover his health,
While Godse reached there with a wrong will
With twenty youths by a bus for his faith;
They chanted anti-slogans and stood still.

Gandhi called him to discuss if any jot,
But Godse refused to talk to Him;
In the evening, moving with knife to hurt,
Manishankar and Bhilare caught him.

Bhilare also finds recorded his statement
Before "Kapoor Commission" appointed
In the Gandhi murder case, later by the goverment.
This shows the mindset of Godse as he did.

Godse, a man ready to kill such a man,
Who is recovering from an ailment, then?

Daggerism

So many people believe in daggerism
To fulfil their aim in a bloody way;
Quite out of any established realism
And too able to send anything to clay.

It can easily cut the roots of religion,
That is the mission of someone to flame –
That can ruin or waste any good mission –
Firmly believing that no one can blame.

Daggerism means total decay of the world –
Daggerism means no religion in the world –
Daggerism means no humanity in the world
Where all things are blotted and curled.

Annihilation is born from its womb;
Now the nonviolent arm can only comb.

The Earth Knows

Nineteen twenty-five, birth in Nagpur;
The impetus to provide goodness
Through Hindu discipline to make it better
And to unite Hindus for better-ness.

The motive behind all this of its troop?
For forming a great Hindu nation?
But for whom? For the marginalised group?
Does the Earth Mother know them and their passion?

Which admired Hitler and Mussolini
During the fire of the Second World War?
Which supported the Jewish state, then ruin? –
And rejected Gandhi's willingness so far?

Then only one who did participate –
Others were doing it for gain or to bet?

Do You Do the Same?

In nineteen hundred fifteen waves;
Saying to work with Hindus' concurrence.
Any help to the work against the Raj days?
Abstained the Civil Disobedience?

Joined hands with the League's main
And other parties; governments of the coalition;
Joining Sindh, passed the first resolution
For creating Pakistan, a new nation.

Governments in Bengal with then Fazlul Haq;
With Khan in North West Frontier Province;
Khanna became a minister in its sake;
What of the Quit India Movement to a fence?

A letter to work for defeating them;
Agreed with Jinnah's gain, not India's fame.

Who Are True Patriots?

Who jumped into the water of the sea?
Who begs pardon for clemency?
Who changes the name of the book writer?
Who wrote twenty-two letters for release?

They said he was gallant – a hero, who tends.
They said he was a patriot or a being.
Know who is a patriot? Who surrenders?
Who begs pardon, or who struggles lifelong?

Mandela never urged for his release;
Three thousand five hundred and twenty-nine days –
Nine times in jail, but by Nehru no urge
Gandhi never, though thirteen times in age.

Jatin never said, though, sixty-nine days fasting.
Who killed Truth in the temple, is a man great?

The Indian National Congress

The birth of the Congress, Hume – the President,
Which began to work hard for nourishment
Of mother India and to improve it
And to settle the work for betterment.

Started Indian civil disobedience –
And the Quit India Movement for Freedom –
Also supported the Khilafat once –
And held the Salt Satyagraha without an atom.

At the Round Table Conferences, it held –
The ethos of nonviolence to release –
For the power transfer, it also moved –
Works against untouchability in gross.

It washed the black blots of thousands of years
And placed India under bliss, with no fears.

Who Created Pakistan?

The two-nation theory declared who
In Ahmedabad in nineteen thirty-seven
Before the proposal of the League, to grow?
Does it show? Did they make India heaven?

These two said nationalists always worked
Against one another and created problems.
In "Quit India" they never participated
And wrote to the Raj, for the power creams?

That they did not support the movement?
Who wrote a letter to Hitler and he greeted?
All knew it, so the Raj did not arrest
As all was meaningless and darted.

Who soared that only Hindus would rule
Independent India, Muslims not well?

The Spinning Wheel

The cause of India's poverty, Gandhi felt,
This was due to the destruction of weaving
And the then-British rule, which broadly dealt
With the main motive to carry to leaving.

Gandhi said to take up the handloom
To save the country from destruction,
That was for Him the employment balm –
That would be for India's construction.

He set up handlooms accordingly.
Maganlal and several others learned fast weaving
Gandhi enjoyed it phenomenally –
Telling his aides to increase spinning.

It became very popular across the country;
For employment, it was revolutionary.

Ifs and Buts

Futile to argue in terms of ifs and buts –
It is faulty to say anything to halt –
It would have been better if such and such dates –
A thing had been done for the secured cult.

In such and such a way to secure target –
One should do anything only in God's name
And should not argue anything to bait,
But should express in very straight fame.

In real life, many people commit mistakes
And try to justify their bad deeds for fame.
Indeed, all these are unjustified shapes
Everyone should recognize the claim.

Oh! Ifs and buts are always to misguide
And someone keeps bad habits not to guide.

Thought as Action

Thought and action are two different things –
Thought as action is the true thought as a lamp
Thought without action is meaningless –
Thought with action is really brought up.

Aha! One who attains that power in life –
One who acts and proceeds as per one's thought,
He's far away from illusion or strife
Like any lesson of goodwill can be taught.

One who delivers a good lecture on the stage,
But works to gain according to himself;
Really an evil manufacturer of sage
And thus stocks sin on his character shelf.

Very few people act according to life
While many moves and handle to keep all safe.

The Unusual Remedy

If Gandhi got the shivers on wintry nights;
He would find relief through one of His aides;
A woman beside Him for winter fights;
When assailed in the trembling insides.

This was an unusual remedy for Him
As He sometimes suffer'd from such a fit;
When in tension or in seriousness beam;
When He sometimes felt severe pain in His waist.

As David was unable to feel any warmth,
Though fully covered at night with some clothes
And when young Abhisag was brought for cloth,
Who cherish'd the king, administered to his colds?

Gandhi's practice or remedy in full knowledge
Of Kasturba, and not a matter of rage.

Simplicity and Artificiality

Gandhi passed His whole life quite simply;
He was away from artificiality;
His food was simple and worked amply;
In his whole life, He followed divinity.

He condensed modern artificiality
Of so call'd civilized life in the world;
Can't have any accord with true simplicity
Of heart to be flourish'd or to be glad.

As life simple is, proceeds towards truth –
As artificial is, moves towards evil;
Who is cross-exercised only for mirth;
He practised his whole life as a devil.

So simplicity is one of the virtues
Artificiality is evil, all views.

The Roots of Religion

Each religion has truth and untruth;
The roots of religions are one, and pure;
All come from the same source as faith.
Hence all are equal; all roots are sure.

Non-violence, truth, non-stealing, chastity
Non-possession, labour, control of the palate,
Fearlessness at all times and touching duty,
Swadeshi, and for all, equal respect.

All these should be observed in life
As possible in our daily work,
Otherwise, religion would become unsafe
As they are true associates to book.

Love, brotherhood, compassion, and tolerance,
Sympathy, mercy, and cooperation, they must be our senses.

Religion and Social Service

The religion of humanity is best;
And can be done through truth and non-violence;
That is love, in a sense the broadest;
Truth is God, and God is Truth in Gandhi's sense.

The denial of Truth, the denial of God,
That is unfelt by us in our daily life
That brings us to dirty ground;
That is irreligious and all round rife.

Human beings are all sparks of truth;
The total sum of it's indescribable,
As yet unknown Truth, that is God, is Faith;
All this in social life is bearable.

Escape from social service is untruth;
Beyond it, there is no joy on the earth.

Truth through Love

Truth and love are guides of human beings.
Only through it, God can be defined;
Impossible to reach Him except for these doings;
Except through true love, can it be found?

Love can only be expressed fully
When man reduces himself to a cipher.
This should be the human's effort only;
It is the only effort for the worth-maker.

It's possible only through self-restraint,
Which is ever-increasing for gaining.
If a man has an ego of one's state or is faint,
This is no love, but only bargaining.

To find the truth, true love should be moved;
If love is moved, the divine is shocked.

Works Against Untouchability

In the full Congress session of Nagpur –
In nineteen hundred and eighteen
Gandhi moved a resolution to cure –
To cure the class, that was depressed within.

This was the first time in history
That a voice was raised against the evil
And was made in Congress mandatory
To abolish the evil – to make it nil.

He made it a regular programme
And held many meetings for its removal.
Dining with untouchables for balm;
They were allowed to enter the school.

He worked for them until His last breath
Who were in Indian society beneath.

Nursing a Leper

Shastri for his entry to the Ashram,
Who's a leper and a Sanskrit scholar
After being shunned everywhere in shame;
Ask'd for permission to live and die there.

Gandhi admitted Shastri to the Ashram,
Not to die, but rather to pass his life in peace
He felt the Ashram of the best frame
And for service a place without price.

A small hut was built for him near Gandhi's place
Where Gandhi regularly nursed and massaged.
He improved for a while at the place,
But later, ultimately succumbed.

A great man whose religion was service
A man who did not fail to do this.

Atom Bomb and Gandhi's View

"Jews had been cruelly wrong'd on Palestine place –
A deep and dark blot on the Christian world.
The bomb has deadened the finest in grace
Which was sustain'd for ages for mankind."

"The laws of war which made it tolerable.
Now we know the naked truth of it all.
War knows no law except that of able
It crushes love, truth, and peace to fall."

"If atomic energy is utilized for good
Of mankind, nothing is wrong with it.
But if it is for crushing truth or need,
It's entirely religiously unfit."

"Only evil can come out of evil
As does good out of good, and not the devil."

Princely States

The Princely State issue could turn India
Into a battleground – a civil war.
So Gandhi cast a steady eye on this idea;
Not a ruler, but people had to clear.

Hyderabad or Junagarh had the wrong will
Or of the Kashmir, same policy, as ample.
Phizo met Him and said of Naga's to derail,
But He said the isolation was impossible.

He met Hari, his wife, Ramchadra and Begam
Also visited Hindus and six refugee camps;
Consoled them as then none like Him,
Who could turn war into peace and courtships.

Thus, the demand for the Princely States
Was completely out of the rulers' hearts.

A vision of Free India

In Panchgani, He drew a look at free India
Where the last is equal to the first
Or none is to be the first or last idea;
Right to equality was of the best rate.

"Independence must begin at the bottom;
Every village will be a republic
With an ever-widening circle of freedom;
Life will not be a pyramid, but classic."

"It will not be an oceanic mileage,
Whose centre will be the individual?
Always ready to perish for the village –
Never aggressive, but ever humble."

"Shar'ng the majesty of the oceanic circle
Of which they are units quite integral."

The Last Birthday

The last birthday of nineteen forty-seven
Came to Him for revision of His stay
On Earth, then, to continue His mission
To other countries and to delay.

All the people present there were shocked
To listen to the thrilling words of Gandhi
That it was His last birthday and time to go
After His mission; and was heard by fellow.

Some remembered His idea to live long –
For a full one hundred and twenty-five years
To wash away the existing working
While there were a number of His dears.

He did not want to be a witness to this,
Practis'd around, He wanted to miss.

Gandhi Wants to Leave the World

He showered with every breath possible
For soon breaking up the chains of slavery
Of India to restore peace and justice as able
To work for humanity with bravery.

After freedom, no peace or fraternity
Several people took part in the riots
Without thinking anything of chastity
Forgetting Azad and Bhagat Singh's hot fights.

He didn't want to witness this
As He expected to maintain full peace;
And if not possible by Him ready to miss
There was a fire in freedom's service.

So Gandhi desired to leave the world
So not the world of darkness to behold.

On the Day of the Assassination

Alas! Patel with his daughter Maniben met Him
On the very day of the assassination
And communicated his message to fame –
About the then issues in the nation.

His relationship with Nehru during his reign
Which was disliked by Patel at that time –
Gandhi wanted to control the condition
About some new issues in His prime.

He told Patel to wait for only a day
Because Nehru had also to meet Him there
To discuss the same issues on the way.
So, Patel went and Gandhi moved for the prayer.

But He was ten minutes late to reach
And He moved fast to the seat to preach.

From the Prayer

He lived and worked only for others;
He did nothing for Himself in any way
He was not like others, who bothers,
Who could easily turn dark night into day?

All over the world, He's quite matchless;
No one could touch His achievement height;
Obviously, in all ways, He was for grace,
Who ate to live, He simplified His diet.

"O Merciful God of Gods I need nothing;
I, neither for heaven nor for the kingdom;
Neither for liberation nor anything;
Only to end the woes of men; to end the shame."

He begged pardon for errors of hand,
Foot, ears, eyes, commission-omission in mind.

Three Cotton Slabs

Using three cotton slabs to assassinate
While Gandhi stopped all in His body.
None was harassed by Him anyway to date –
All were moved by His mark fully ready.

Godse did, but himself kill'd while living –
Gandhi died, but still alive in our hearts.
Godse survived, but for the time being
While Gandhi's immortal in our deep cults.

People knew to think the deed of Godse
That he did only to blame the root
While some others supported such a way –
The way of full bloodshed, violence, and dirt.

Gandhi is alive while physically dead;
Godseism is dead as it itself has held.

Shame, Shame, Shame!

Shame, the people who undertook such a blotted deed!
Shame, such deed which was quite out-rooted!
Shame, such ideology that placed Him dead!
Shame, such organizations which powered!

Who assassinat'd the Father of the Nation –
The Citizen of the World and the Saint,
While His hands were armless to pray then –
While answering the greetings He then bent.

Bravery or cowardice the people know,
Who were with gun-cotton slabs on the site;
Where Gandhi was there in a row to vow;
While they were all for their communal fight.

Such a black deed never in history
And the dust knows Godseism's mystery.

Ram! Ram!

As Gandhi proceeded to the lectern white,
Godse came and bent as to touch His feet
"O brother, leave the way; He's already late,"
But he began to fire on Him for death's visit.

The words of "Ram…Ram" at last came from Him
When Godse shot three times at His warm body
In the gesture of greetings from the heart beam;
And left the woeful world which was muddy.

Fell down on the shoulders of Abha to rest –
Manu kept Him in her lap when He fell down.
Godse stood there and asked for arrest
As His deed was bloody as felt his own.

Thus, Gandhi left the world having brought freedom
As was possible only by His wisdom.

Speak Bapu, Speak!

Godse shot at the body of Gandhi three times;
He was fully in a gesture of greetings
With both hands in the formal Hindu pastimes
As He was then in spiritual doings.

Three cotton slabs of Godse He stopped;
He fell down on the shoulders of His kith
Keeping His head in her lap she sobbed
Said, "Speak, Bapu, speak" but He embraced death.

After ten minutes in hospital,
He was declared dead with weep'ng compassion;
Became the prey of a deadly ideal,
Which was only one in its core fashion.

After His departure all round darkness;
The end of His nonviolence and kindness.

Bapu No More, But His Light

Men for Gandhi's arrival in the Birla House,
The fatal Friday of hellish January
Of nineteen forty-eight to bounce the sins –
Godse and his members are present in fury.

People for His arrival to deliver –
To express immortal words to the world –
To light the darkness – to turn and clear –
To clear the sins of Mother India's field.

He reached some minutes late to debate;
For universal rebate – for rest and peace;
To clear all woes and sorrows for chaste.
Each one in tears and Mountbatten in grace.

Nehru said, "Now our loving Bapu is no more,
But His light will be with us forever."

The Funeral March

About nine to ten from the Birla House way;
The border of Yamuna where He was cremat'd.
About five hours' time to reach the clay
As all mankind reached and participated.

Men of many castes, colours, and religions;
Both men and women witness the rite;
Leaders, monarchs, officers, and many a one
In anger, woes, and sorrows to rate.

The largest crowd of the funeral march;
And people's eyes flowed with hot tears;
They sat on the mud round the pyre to torch
So none could push it, as all were dears.

They expect'd to fire before the sun set –
To send Gandhi's five elements to their fate.

Gandhi's Cremation

His cremation was held on the thirty-first
On the Rajghat with state salutation;
At the funeral several took part.
How pathetic and miserable was the condition!

Manu placed her head on Sardar Patel's lap –
Wept and wept while He was to put to fire
And there was none to fill His gap –
The people had kept Him on the pyre.

For His permanent loss, people were weeping –
India wept bitterly for her loss –
Rivers and mountains were fully writhing.
It seemed that sin of the world to cross.

His loss was the loss of divinity,
That thrilled even the Himalayan unity.

Now No Claim!

With Gandhi's elements were ready to flame on the pyre
Ramdas put fire to His wooden pyre
To show his claim that He's not his father,
But in fact, earth, water, fire, sky, and air.

When the pyre was in full flame without claim,
"Gandhi Ji Amar Rahe!" People shouted a slogan.
Then there was neither Bapu, nor living fame!
Everything looked unrest born.

Many women tried to jump into the flame –
To be "sati" – to be His part forever,
Only because of His welfare works claim,
But people stopped them from doing so there.

All night people bent their heads in flame,
And on the morning, Nehru put flowers' fame.

Gandhi Ever Relevant

His ideals are immortal and relevant –
Only one propagandized all this
While others doing all this never meant
And in their real-life practice they too miss.

Love, peace, truth, and non-violence are well-known –
Its values are known to shine e'en in the tempest,
Which are priceless and never are blown;
Which should be continued without rest.

These are the roots of all religions
Which are able to further the world,
Otherwise, would be wasted without visions.
So all must strengthen goodness, must behold.

Only His ideals can maintain peace everywhere;
Otherwise, bloodshed and violence with a dare.

India Weeps

The whole earth weeps after His departure;
The highest Himalayas began to melt too;
Holy Ganges thrilled after His murder;
Kaveri had become dry as was no one.

People shivered at His assassination;
The sun became cold for some time;
The moon went hot after Godse's fascination;
The shining stars had lost their prime.

The Holy Earth began to weep for her loss;
All singing forests lost their greenery;
Rivers became totally free from moss;
Sweet fruits turned into a sour adversary.

The greatest man of the world returned;
Oh! After Him, everything was turned.

Excuse Them

A follower of truth and non-violence
Quite against eye for eye justice –
Against blood for blood or the revenging lance;
Against revenge policy for its price.

After His assassination, some men,
Godse and Apte, were sentenced to death
While Manilal and Ramdas said to pardon
As Gandhi was against the loss of Faith.

They began a movement to protect them
And pleaded too, that He was against it
As *"revenge is neither justice nor fame"*.
Their sentence for their deed did not fit.

The government refused clemency
As of deeds of the ideology fancy.